Zero into Four

A Philosophical Drama in 3 Acts

Rajeshwar Prasad

TSL Drama

First published in Great Britain in 2022
By TSL Publications, Rickmansworth

Copyright © 2022 Rajeshwar Prasad

ISBN / 978-1-914245-60-2

Cover image: Rajeshwar Prasad

Zero into Four

Characters

JAMES	16, AMOL's friend, student
AMOL	16, JAMES' friend, student
TARA	30, maid servant at the school
ZARA	38, JAMES' mother

Setting

Act 1
Break time at school under the trees
Act 2
Break time at school under the trees
Act 3
A room in James' home

Running time

Approx 62 minutes

Act 1

Lights up.

JAMES *is sitting under a tree eating sweet-porridge with potato and cauliflower.* AMOL *is sitting under another tree in the school playground. He is muttering and weeping quietly. Other children are eating or playing during the recess.*

JAMES: [*Muttering alone*] Really, very tasty food! How my mother cooks such tasty food! A mother is the heaven of heavens for every child. My dad never gives all this. My dad never says but my mother asks me daily what I want to eat and I say whatever I like. Firstly, I will eat two porridges and then sweet-porridge. I tell her the same every day. How much my mother loves me! How much passion of love and mercy is on me!

AMOL: [*Weeping quietly. Muttering. Eyes full of tears. No voice. Trying to hide and wipe tears with his handkerchief. Sighs very deeply. Heartbroken.*] Oh! Oh! How unjust You are! O my God! [*Looks up to the sky.*]

JAMES: [*Muttering*] Perhaps, AMOL is weeping.

AMOL: [*Muttering*] How unjust You are! O my God!

JAMES: Perhaps! [*Looks at* AMOL. *Tries to assess his condition. Gets up to go to* AMOL.]

AMOL: [*Covering his face with handkerchief. Muttering.*] O God, open Your eyes on me. How helpless I am here in this world. My dad is dying. Now he is my mother too, but he has no breasts to be suckled by my little brother. How much more of my mother's work can my father do! Please. My God! Turn my father into a mother so that he can do all that was done by her. Please make him two in one – father and mother too.

JAMES: [*Moves to* AMOL.] My friend, are you weeping?

~5~

AMOL:	[*weeping. Doesn't speak.*]
JAMES:	[*Takes his head, sitting on the ground and wipes away his tears.*] Dear Amol, why are you weeping?
AMOL:	[*Weeps bitterly. Doesn't speak.*]
JAMES:	Tell me, my friend. Why are you weeping?
AMOL:	[*Continues to weep.*]
JAMES:	[*Giving* AMOL *some sweet-porridge by holding it to his mouth.*] Tell me, my dear friend. Take it and eat.
AMOL:	[*Continues to weep.*]
JAMES:	Why do you not take it? Is it too sweet?
AMOL:	[*weeping*] I will not eat.
JAMES:	Why?
AMOL:	Nothing is sweet.
JAMES:	Why are you sad, Amol? Why weep so?
AMOL:	[*sadly*] Nothing.
JAMES:	Please tell me, Amol.
AMOL:	[*sadly*] Nothing.
JAMES:	Have you eaten?
AMOL:	No.
JAMES:	Why not?
AMOL:	It is not to me.
JAMES:	Why?
AMOL:	Today I could not bring anything.
JAMES:	Why?
AMOL:	It was not cooked.
JAMES:	Why?
AMOL:	My father is ill – he is in a critical condition and is in bed.
JAMES:	What happened to him?
AMOL:	He has been suffering from jaundice for months.

JAMES:	From jaundice?
AMOL:	Yes.
JAMES:	The same disease which causes eyes to become pale?
AMOL:	Yes.
JAMES:	[*Pause*] Oh!
AMOL:	[*Pause*] Not only the eyes, but the whole body. The whole world is pale.
JAMES:	It's a very dangerous disease. So, please care for him.
AMOL:	He's under the treatment of a famous doctor.
JAMES:	Good doctor?
AMOL:	Yes. All say he is the world's greatest doctor.
JAMES:	What is his condition?
AMOL:	Stable.
JAMES:	What does the doctor says?
AMOL:	Fifty-fifty.
JAMES:	Not very good.
AMOL:	[*Silent*]
JAMES:	[*pause*] You should stay and look after him.
AMOL:	I do but he says he will stay alone at home to rest and says I must attend school so that there may not be any loss. So, I have come here leaving my dad. He gave me light snacks in the morning.
JAMES:	Why do you not get your mother to cook food?
AMOL:	[*Silent*]
JAMES:	Why?
AMOL:	[*Very sad with tears in eyes.*] She is gone.
JAMES:	From the world?
AMOL:	No.
JAMES:	Where?
AMOL:	From the roots of values and virtues.
JAMES:	Where?
AMOL:	Quite out from the worldly values and virtues.

JAMES:	How?
AMOL:	Breaking all the established chains and settings which are in favour of mankind for which we always pine and move ahead – and that which always come along the way to help without any cost.
JAMES:	How has she done all this?
AMOL:	With the help of evil, lust and greed – with the help of her well-wishers, parents, brothers and sisters.
JAMES:	Has your mother some such men too?
AMOL:	Yes. All have such men and women.
JAMES:	Yes?
AMOL:	Yes … yes. Many more!
JAMES:	Is your father not alive? As I feel …
AMOL:	He is alive.
JAMES:	Of course?
AMOL:	Yes. Of course!
JAMES:	She should not do this.
AMOL:	But she did. This was natural for her. She used to beat me and my brother.
JAMES:	Don't take it otherwise. All mothers do this for building the character of their children. So, take it as a blessing.
AMOL:	No … no. That is not the matter. The real matter is that she wanted to be free from me so she could enjoy her life freely. I was a burden on her. I was one of the obstructions in her life. So, she divorced me.
JAMES:	What type of woman she is? How does she do all this?
AMOL:	Shamelessly.
JAMES:	Has she not shame?
AMOL:	Not one jot of shame.
JAMES:	What type of mother is she?
AMOL:	Like all others.
JAMES:	No.
AMOL:	I am quite right. It is true. I have seen it.

JAMES:	But my findings are different.
AMOL:	You are in the darkness of ignorance.
JAMES:	I am quite right.
AMOL:	You do not know my mother.
JAMES:	I know my mother, who is full of compassion, love, sympathy and mercy for me and also for my brothers and sisters.
AMOL:	Really, you are far from the truth. The fact is that all these emotions are not in the world. So, where does your mother get these?
JAMES:	What do you mean?
AMOL:	I say that which is quite right. The word has nothing in its name. Mother is nothing. It is merely an illusion.
JAMES:	Think a little. What are you saying?
AMOL:	I witness all this. We all see it in our lives, but forget because of the fat layers of illusion.
JAMES:	But you have never said any of this previously? Suddenly, your opinion has changed.
AMOL:	Previously, I was like you in a state of illusions. I saw when my mother divorced me and told me to live alone in my own way.
JAMES:	Has your mother really divorced you?
AMOL:	Yes, she divorced me along with my brother and father. Now my father cares for us. He plays two roles – one of father – and second of mother.
JAMES:	When did she divorce you?
AMOL:	Months ago.
JAMES:	During the period of your dad's ailment?
AMOL:	Yes.
JAMES:	Why?
AMOL:	She decided to break the illusion – all worldly ties.
JAMES:	What really happened to her?
AMOL:	Nothing happened to her. All this is natural. She simply broke all the ties made by man. She is now living freely.

	She says that life controlled by values and virtues is meaningless.
JAMES:	But we all follow and develop values and virtues.
AMOL:	We follow all this – we further all this – but this is manmade. Therefore, it is artificial and will be ruined one day.
JAMES:	Everything in this world is of man and for man.
AMOL:	But in any situation man moves towards the natural passions.
JAMES:	[*pause*] What?
AMOL:	She believes and advocates life without any worldly ties.
JAMES:	Life without ties?
AMOL:	Yes.
JAMES:	Has she gone mad?
AMOL:	No. She is fine.
JAMES:	[*pause*] How does she live?
AMOL:	Have you seen feral animals like the dog, pig, cat etc?
JAMES:	Several times.
AMOL:	In the same way.
JAMES:	In the very way?
AMOL:	Yes … yes.
JAMES:	Does she live as an animal?
AMOL:	Yes. Freely.
JAMES:	But how does she do it? This is a big issue.
AMOL:	No. It is natural.
JAMES:	What?
AMOL:	I know it without doubt. All mothers are the same.
JAMES:	No.
AMOL:	I see – I feel. All others see, but ignore.
JAMES:	This is not right. It is something else. There may be one or two women like this, but others are compassionate.

AMOL:	I tell you, no mother is compassionate.
JAMES:	All! All!
AMOL:	None.
JAMES:	All are compassionate as I far as I see. Their faces are in the food of our lunch boxes which they packed. This shows love and compassion for their children. This shows their motherly touch. Only mothers can do this.
AMOL:	No.
JAMES:	What, not?
AMOL:	It's an illusion.
JAMES:	It is fact.
AMOL:	No. You don't know the truth.
JAMES:	I know all.
AMOL:	You know nothing.
JAMES:	You must try to know them before ill-speaking.
AMOL:	I know them. I am not ill-speaking them but I say what I find and see – which all see and face.
JAMES:	You are not right in this regard. All are not like your mother.
AMOL:	Ignorant James! I also used to say and think that my mother was compassionate, loved me with every breath of her life. But now my ideas and faith have been shattered – my dreams have been ruined – I have come to see reality. Now I know that the concept of mother and motherhood is absolutely false.
JAMES:	It seems you are a mother-hater.
AMOL:	No ... no.
JAMES:	Why not?
AMOL:	This is not a matter. The fact is that I respect mothers saying 'mama ... aunt'. I hate no mother. I love them all ... I honour them all.

JAMES:	If you love them or respect them, your opinion should be different.
AMOL:	I can never make mistakes. I am quite right. There is nothing in its name. 'Mother', the word is itself a non-existentialistic word.
JAMES:	You don't understand the main point of mother and motherhood.
AMOL:	Know ... know! The idea of mother and motherhood is quite false.
JAMES:	Entirely?
AMOL:	Yes ... yes.
JAMES:	How?
AMOL:	There is no mother. There is only one mother.
JAMES:	Who?
AMOL:	The earth mother.
JAMES:	Who has given birth to us?
AMOL:	The earth mother – to melt into the earth mother – to join the earth mother after death.
JAMES:	Has the earth mother given birth to us?
AMOL:	Yes.
JAMES:	Yes?
AMOL:	Yes ... yes.
JAMES:	How?
AMOL:	Elements into elements – zero into four – earth into earth. We all are the same. We are made of only four elements – although Indians say that man is made of five elements – earth, water, fire, sky and air.
JAMES:	Elements?
AMOL:	Yes ... yes. We are made of four elements: earth, water, fire, and air.
JAMES:	I have seen this type of programme on television. The saint was delivering this idea and said that the body is

made of four elements and after death it changes into all this. Then there is no existence of our body.

AMOL: Quite right!

JAMES: But there is a great difference between mother and the earth.

AMOL: What?

JAMES: The earth is inanimate and mother is living. We are living. So, we all are of mothers, not of the earth. Although people say that our greater mother is the earth.

AMOL: Of course! We all are followers of 'zero into four' – 'earth, water, fire and air'.

JAMES: Yes. I used to listen to it frequently but I ignore this stupid idea now.

AMOL: No one can ignore it. This is man's eternal bond and no one can break it under any condition. This is entirely beyond the reach of man.

JAMES: [*silent*]

AMOL: There is no mother in the cosmos – man is of 'zero into four', by 'zero into four', and for 'zero into four'.

JAMES: Where did you learn all this?

AMOL: I see this on the eternal television screen entitled 'zero into four'.

JAMES: [*silent*]

AMOL: Do you not see it?

JAMES: No. I don't.

AMOL: All see.

JAMES: No ... no.

AMOL: Believe. All see even if their eyes are closed.

JAMES: What do you say?

AMOL: I say what I see on the screen and what is said by the eternal deliverer.

JAMES:	Who?
AMOL:	Eternal deliverer.
JAMES:	Who?
AMOL:	Nature.
JAMES:	Nature is the eternal deliverer?
AMOL:	Yes.
JAMES:	How?
AMOL:	See the programme and you will know.
JAMES:	Where?
AMOL:	Where all see.
JAMES:	On the screen?
AMOL:	Yes, on the earth screen.
JAMES:	I see like others. But in spite of this I can't say that my mother is the earth. My mother is full of love and compassion, but the earth mother has no such emotion.
AMOL:	[*laughs*] Ha ... ha ... ha!
JAMES:	Why?
AMOL:	The passion and feeling which is shown by mothers are false. The time comes when all this is ignored by them and they adopt the law of Nature. She deals with us as Nature. I am one of its examples. My mother is a great example of all this.
JAMES:	Think a little.
AMOL:	I think about it – I consider it seriously. All say the same. In my village there is a popular song which is sung by all children which shows the truth of mother.
JAMES:	Which song?
AMOL:	It begins with 'mother is ...'
JAMES:	Please sing it.
AMOL:	Listen.

Sings.

Mother too is false.
The earth is her base,
An idea to be fun,
But felt by none.

Mother too is false.
She is really to pose,
And sinks like the sun –
Making man's life fun.

Mother too is false.
Man is only for loss.
Leaving all in vain –
Everyone, not only one.

Mother too is false.
But seems as a rose –
Not any compassion
Man's life is fiction.

JAMES: [*laughs*] Ha ... ha!

AMOL: Why do you laugh?

JAMES: Who composed this song?

AMOL: This is not a human-created song.

JAMES: Who composed it?

AMOL: This is a natural song which has been sung across ages – generation to generation.

JAMES: Really, a very stupid song?

AMOL: Really, a song which presents a true picture of mother! Believe me!

JAMES: [*long pause*] Let it go. Please tell me. What has really happened to your mother?

AMOL: None can let go. All learn. All embrace. All welcome it.

JAMES: But let it go.

AMOL: Okay.

JAMES: Tell me.

AMOL:	She was quite loveless, merciless and compassionless. She behaved as a machine.
JAMES:	A mother can't be a machine. I don't believe it.
AMOL:	Believe it!
JAMES:	You are wrong.
AMOL:	Believe me!
JAMES:	It is quite impossible that a mother can be a machine and that she loses the emotion of love and compassion for her children.
AMOL:	But my mother is quite free from any sense of love and compassion. She has nothing of its kind.
JAMES:	Know! Your mother is unique. But others are different. Whether she is like others or not it is a matter of study. But I believe she is also like others.
AMOL:	You don't know many mothers. All are the same. All follow the formula of 'zero into four'.
JAMES:	Never?
AMOL:	Never!
JAMES:	This is really, very shocking.
AMOL:	Whatever it is, but I say what I see and what I face.
JAMES:	But ...
AMOL:	Believe.
JAMES:	Has she divorced your father too?
AMOL:	Not only my father, but also my brother and me.
JAMES:	Now where does she live?
AMOL:	She lives wherever she feels.
JAMES:	Does she see you occasionally?
AMOL:	Never.
JAMES:	Never?
AMOL:	Really, never!
JAMES:	Does she meet your dad?

AMOL:	Never.
JAMES:	Have you contacted her since?
AMOL:	Not directly, but by telephone.
JAMES:	Has she asked about you?
AMOL:	No.
JAMES:	What does she say?
AMOL:	She asks me why I contacted her?
JAMES:	What do you reply?
AMOL:	I ask her to continue providing her love and mercy for me and my younger brother – for my dad, who is now in a miserable condition.
JAMES:	Does she want to come to you?
AMOL:	Never.
JAMES:	Is she not in a situation to show her love and compassion for you all?
AMOL:	Not in this miserable condition.
JAMES:	Has she no love and mercy?
AMOL:	She has no love, mercy or any other compassion.
JAMES:	A unique situation.
AMOL:	It's natural!
JAMES:	Unnatural!
AMOL:	Know. Very, very natural!
JAMES:	Previously?
AMOL:	In the past, her love and mercy were also artificial. She used to sugar-coat everything, only to misguide me, while she was in search of time to be free from the clutches of every tie and when such time came she broke all ties fully. Now she lives freely following 'zero into four'.
JAMES:	You should go to her.

AMOL:	If I go, she will have me killed. She will not accept any ties. I am a burden for her. She has tried to kill my dad several times already.
JAMES:	[*pause*] Oh! How does she live?
AMOL:	She lives naturally.
JAMES:	You should win her heart using 'mama ... mama' words very sweetly. In this way, she can surrender before you and you will be once again be flooded with motherly love and mercy.
AMOL:	She was always false.
JAMES:	You are wrong.
AMOL:	I am right.
JAMES:	You should see me. How much love and mercy I gain from my mother! [*Shows chocolate, biscuits and new garments which he is wearing.*]
AMOL:	[*weeps. Sad.*] All this is meaningless. She has openly said to me that she is not my mother – think and live alone. She says she is not to look back and she will continue to do what now she is doing.
JAMES:	It really is a unique condition.
AMOL:	I know. I face it. All face it at some stage of life.
JAMES:	Really, very unique.
AMOL:	It is not unique but natural. All do the same. All break the tie once the time comes. All live under illusion but the fact is that all are the same. There is no mother who has true love except the earth mother that invites all to join and be part of. Nature loves us well and never divorces anyone. She welcomes us warmly and we all join happily or unhappily.
JAMES:	You constantly blur the facts and are never serious about getting her love, so she stays away.
AMOL:	You misunderstand.

JAMES:	You can win her heart by showing her true love. Love can win the world, not only your mother. So try to win her using human passion and emotion. I am sure, she will come back to you and you will enjoy motherly love as I enjoy it.
AMOL:	All this is an illusion. I will not again become the victim of such illusions. Now I have overcome this state of illusion, I am free from such expectations.
JAMES:	But that is not all. There is something more you must consider.
AMOL:	I have considered all this very deeply – I have witnessed all this very clearly.
JAMES:	Think and try to know some other mothers.
AMOL:	I am absolutely accurate. I know it well.
JAMES:	Stop and think, move on. Why is your mother not coming to you?
AMOL:	She has very openly said that she can come to us, but she will remain free to do whatever she wishes – she can go anywhere at any time – she can go with anyone and no one will obstruct her. She says that if we agree to all this, she is ready to come and live with us.
JAMES:	Why does she want all this to be done?
AMOL:	She wants to be free from family commitment and to live freely.
JAMES:	Are all facilities available to your family or not?
AMOL:	Each and every modern facility is available.
JAMES:	Then why does she do this?
AMOL:	She says that all are naturally free, so she is also free following 'zero into four'.
JAMES:	Does she lack morality?
AMOL:	Yes ... yes.
JAMES:	This is very wrong. She should look at the world and its people, how they live and maintain relationships.

AMOL:	But all this creates bonds for her.
JAMES:	The sacrifice of her parents is bad, so she does all this.
AMOL:	Yes ... yes. Her parents are far greater than her in this regard. They are a hundred times more than her.
JAMES:	You mean they do the same in a more advanced way?
AMOL:	Yes ... yes. You are right. Her parents encourage her.
JAMES:	How are they?
AMOL:	They are of the same nature. Her sister has did in before and divorced her husband – she divorced all virtues and values.
JAMES:	Her younger sister too?
AMOL:	Yes.
JAMES:	Oh!
AMOL:	Know. Her mother has done the same.
JAMES:	Also her mother?
AMOL:	Yes.
JAMES:	All?
AMOL:	All have done the same!
JAMES:	[astonishingly] All?
AMOL:	Most of her relatives have done the same. They feel this is the life – and life under such values and virtues are man-made – and therefore unnatural. So, they neglect all this and further their mission in the same way.
JAMES:	Has her younger sister really done so?
AMOL:	Yes ... yes. This is very common among her family and relatives.
JAMES:	Has she really divorced her husband?
AMOL:	Twelve years ago she established such records.
JAMES:	And her child?

AMOL:	The child lives with her. Bed to bed a new uncle is gained for the child. Intoxicating medicines are administered to the child. When she sleeps, each deed is done by her and as she can. She does so freely and fearlessly. She feels pleasure saying that her child has gained a new uncle. Hundreds of uncles are gained for the child. People say all this.
JAMES:	[*silent*]
AMOL:	Is this love for the child or has she divorced her? Does she feel happy with the child or does she bear it only to show society?
JAMES:	[*long pause*] Oh! What sacrament is in their family?
AMOL:	You may understand.
JAMES:	Have you not asked her?
AMOL:	No.
JAMES:	You must know.
AMOL:	When some problems occurred, I asked my dad about it. He said all this is common. He mistakenly embraced the wedding tie with her and was fulfilling the social and religious bond which he made in front of thousands of people. He also says that the seven steps around the fire are unforgettable for him and he will never break them.
JAMES:	Which steps?
AMOL:	The seven steps around the fire which he took during his marriage ceremony.
JAMES:	Yes ... yes. I have seen such rituals during the marriage ceremony taken by the bridegroom.
AMOL:	Right you are. My dad remembers and says he needs no pardon because he is right and she is wrong – he has fulfilled his religious duty as promised by him – she has broken the vows, so she will suffer.
JAMES:	But your mother doesn't feel all this?
AMOL:	No.

JAMES:	No?
AMOL:	Really ... never.
JAMES:	Is she not afraid of God?
AMOL:	There is no God, so why will be she afraid of Him?
JAMES:	Is there no God?
AMOL:	No.
JAMES:	How?
AMOL:	If there is one, where do you find him? What kind of justice do you see when someone breaks the chains of values and virtues?
JAMES:	But none has the right to question the existence of God.
AMOL:	This is the fact: there is no God in the cosmos. So, it is not wrong to say so.
JAMES:	This is the reason behind your suffering.
AMOL:	Your idea is absolutely absurd.
JAMES:	God is only truth.
AMOL:	Only the concept of 'zero into four' is true.
JAMES:	You are forever trying to pull me towards untruth.
AMOL:	My dad believes in God. But it is quite meaningless. All in vain.
JAMES:	Never. It is only fruitful.
AMOL:	He believes God, but He has awarded him nothing except loss and suffering. I think my dad arrived in this world only for this, though he is very sincere and honest – he is a very religious minded person. For him, values and virtues are everything. He never moves against all this but tries to strengthen it all. He always tries to further moving on the path of righteousness.
JAMES:	[*long pause*] Why does your mother not think of and remember these values and virtues – the seven steps around the fire?

AMOL: She told me about it and remembered too.

JAMES: But why does she not fulfil the promises made by her?

AMOL: She said she remembered but that it was a mockery in the existence of Nature. She said that Nature is everything and she always tries to move on its path.

JAMES: Is she not immoral and pathless?

AMOL: My dad says so. He also points to many scriptures in its favour. He says that she will be penalized by God.

JAMES: Definitely.

AMOL: [*laughs*] Ha ... Ha.

JAMES: Why? This is not a matter to be laughed at.

AMOL: No one will penalize her. No one penalizes Nature. All this is natural. All has the same condition. No one is free of its clutches.

JAMES: This is wholly wrong.

AMOL: It is absolutely right.

JAMES: No.

AMOL: Know it well. Your eyes will be opened in the future. Let the time come.

JAMES: I know and enjoy it too. I know and understand the love and compassion of a mother. So, I have more experiences than others.

AMOL: I want you to know that you are misunderstanding the main point. Go to the past and know and understand all this.

JAMES: What?

AMOL: Previously, I thought the same. But now my condition compels me to think broadly and I find that all are the same and there is no mother.

JAMES: What do you mean to say?

AMOL: There is nothing in the name mother. I know that which has been done by my mother, the same has been done by her sister and her mother. This is inherited. This is natural. She alone is not entitled to this. This is the way of Nature which commands all of us. She is doing no wrong, so no penalty will be pronounced against her. I know it well. All have only to follow 'zero into four'. Either one is right or one is wrong.

JAMES: Has the same been done by her mother?

AMOL: Yes … yes. She is the same. She has done the same and encourages the same.

JAMES: Really, a very delicate condition of the world.

AMOL: Really. Believe. She divorced her husband and lived alone for years. Later, she became pregnant, and therefore she married the man who is now my maternal grandfather. It is known by all the people.

JAMES: In the holy heart of earth, all this is done. This is a matter of shame.

AMOL: No … no. It is not a matter of shame. All this is common. All this is natural.

JAMES: Why not shame?

AMOL: This is a matter of pride for all. See our ten female teachers. Ten out of twelve are divorcees. They feel proud that there is no control. They used to say they did not like to live under any clutches. When their children became adult, they were automatically given to their dads and the mothers lived alone. They were only the means who followed the mode to create them.

JAMES: You always talk unnecessarily. You don't know anything.

AMOL: You don't know.

JAMES: I know well. You mother is different. You all belong to a different sacrament. You all live in another world.

AMOL: No … no.

JAMES: [Gives a toffee to AMOL.] See and eat. Do you know how much my mother loves me? How much compassion she has for me! She gives me all this daily –

at least one special item just for me which I now am giving to you, take it, eat it. It is full of my mother's love. Do you think that my mother is like yours? She is really a mother. She is really like a mother. She is full of all motherly virtues.

AMOL: [*Refuses to take it and begins to weep.*]

JAMES: Take, my friend.

AMOL: [*Continues to weep.*]

JAMES: Silence, my friend. Why are you weeping? I will give you a toffee daily. I will also bring food for you daily. Don't weep. I will share with you your woes and sorrows. Don't worry. Don't remember her. Let her go. Let her divorce. I will tell my mama to adopt you as her son. I will be happy, if she does so. I will tell her to shower love and compassion on you like me. Keep patience. Success is hidden in patience.

AMOL: [*Continues to weep bitterly and says pathetically.*] Your mother will also divorce you one day. You will become like me. I am sure, James. Believe. There is no mother in this world. There is only one mother of all and that is the earth mother, who is the greatest mother.

JAMES: My friend! Will my mother also divorce me? I too think she will leave me one day.

           Begins to weep with him.

Lights down.

Act 2

Lights up.

JAMES and AMOL are weeping bitterly. TARA, a government maid servant of the school, comes to investigate. Her duty includes looking after students. The bell rings.

TARA: What has happened to you, Amol? What has happened to you, James?

AMOL: [*Continues to weep.*]

JAMES: [*Continues to weep.*]

TARA: Shh, Amol. Shh James.

JAMES: [*Weeping.*] Amol is weeping bitterly. His mother has divorced him and his dad too.

TARA: Because of this?

JAMES: Yes.

TARA: Only because of this?

JAMES: Yes. He says that one day my mother will also divorce me. If she does so, what will happen to me and my life? – what will happen to my dad, brothers and sisters? Who will give me food and sweets? My mother loves me too much. She is full of motherly virtues.

AMOL: [*weeping*] I am sure, James. She'll divorce you one day. All divorce. All are alone.

TARA: [*Keeping them close to her.*] Shhh. Listen to me, my boys – listen to me, my sons.

JAMES: [*pathetically*] Aunt, please tell me, will my mother also leave me?

TARA: Never.

AMOL: My aunt! But I have been divorced by my mother, so I think he will also be divorced one day – all will be

~ 26~

divorced. I have seen several times on the television that mother is also under the concept of 'zero into four'.

TARA: You are still young, so you don't understand the real issue. No mother divorces her children. Some mothers divorce their husbands – but very rarely. So, none will divorce you. Keep silent. Go to class. Your teacher is calling. The bell has been rung.

JAMES: My aunt! Will my mother never divorce me?

TARA: Believe me! Never! All mothers love their children. They are full of compassion. The lap of a mother is the second heaven. The same pleasure is found here which we find in heaven. So don't worry.

AMOL: [weeping] But my mother has divorced me. She has forgotten me. She said she is not my mother. She moves freely as the west wind and she has forgotten all values and virtues.

TARA: She has divorced not you, but your dad. Know. Why are you anxious? Why are you weeping?

AMOL: I have seen so many in this very condition. My maternal grandmother has done the same. My dad says that his mother also did so. He has several records.

TARA: Your dad is now frustrated because of the divorce by his wife. So, please don't listen to him on this and continue to study and attend classes.

AMOL: No. He is always happy. He says that this is inherited by all. He has several examples and proof of this type. There are others too in my village who are in the same situation.

TARA: My dear sons! Listen to me please. You are now minors. Why do you think about such issues? When you grow older, you may think all this.

JAMES: [pause] How many children do you have, aunt?

TARA: Four.

JAMES:	Where do they live?
TARA:	In Forgetland.
JAMES:	Where is that?
TARA:	You are minors. You can't understand all this. This is a subject of deep understanding.
JAMES:	I will try.
TARA:	All try, but they never know some places.
JAMES:	I should know all places.
TARA:	Man always tries to know but fails to do so.
JAMES:	Then what happens?
TARA:	Then there is 'zero into four' and all is wasted.
JAMES:	Then?
TARA:	Unknown.
JAMES:	Unknown?
TARA:	Quite unknown!
JAMES:	Then what will occur?
TARA:	All changes into meaninglessness.
JAMES:	Into meaninglessness?
TARA:	Yes.
JAMES:	[Sadly] All this happens?
TARA:	[Slowly] Yes.
JAMES:	Then what will happen to your children?
TARA:	The same.
JAMES:	The same?
TARA:	Yes.
JAMES:	My aunt! Why do they not live with you?
TARA:	They live with their dad and he cares for them.
JAMES:	Why do they not live with you?
TARA:	Their dad is a powerful agency. He commands all. He is like the sun which purifies all. After purification, new

shape is given. It has new customers ... new shops ... new places ... many ... many.

JAMES: Their dad looks after them?

TARA: Yes ... yes.

JAMES: It means you are also free?

TARA: [*Hesitates, slowly.*] Yes.

JAMES: Do you live alone?

TARA: [*Hesitatingly, slowly.*] Y...e...s.

JAMES: Have you divorced them?

TARA: No.

JAMES: Then why do they not live with you?

TARA: They live with their dad.

JAMES: Does their dad love them more than you?

TARA: No.

JAMES: Why do you not keep them with you?

TARA: It is the eternal fact: all have to go to the father. The father always waits for all to come in time and finally all go to him happily or unhappily.

JAMES: But in any situation, you should keep them all.

TARA: No one wants to live with their mother. All want to go to their father.

JAMES: You should care for them. You should give them biscuits and toffees. You should keep them on your lap.

TARA: That is unnatural.

JAMES: Where does the uncle live?

TARA: He also lives in Forgetland.

JAMES: Not with you?

TARA: Now not.

JAMES: Did he live with you in the past?

TARA: Yes.

JAMES:	It means you have divorced him?
TARA:	[*Hesitates*] Yes.
JAMES:	It means now you live alone?
TARA:	[*Hesitatingly, slowly.*] Sometimes, someone lives with me.
JAMES:	Temporarily?
TARA:	Yes.
JAMES:	Why have you divorced him?
TARA:	I don't like him. I feel always lost there. I have tried but all in vain. I used to feel there is nothing to me. There is no one with me. All are alone, whatever I try.
JAMES:	Even with your children, do you not feel wanted?'
TARA:	Never.
JAMES:	Never?
TARA:	Really … never.
JAMES:	Are they not liked by you?
TARA:	I liked them. I loved them. But I used to feel all this as a bond. I want to be free from all the clutches of the world. I feel that everything in the world is false. I am alone here and my life is meaningless.
AMOL:	[*Long pause*] The aunt is right. She is quite right and always speaks the truth. I also have the same feelings and experiences. I have seen many divorced men and women living alone.
TARA:	[*Silent*]
AMOL:	No mother loves their children. They try to keep their children away from them. They weep and cry like me. Some mothers move on the bank of the river at midnight and they administer sleeping pills to their children to sleep. All mothers are loveless and merciless.
TARA:	[*long pause*] All this is common. Don't think about it.

AMOL:	If I am right, ten out of twelve of our female teachers are divorcees?
TARA:	All are divorcees.
AMOL:	All?
TARA:	All ... all!
AMOL:	But people say that ten among twelve?
TARA:	Ten have divorced and the other two are in the process. The matter is under the consideration of their fathers. Dads will have to decide – and the decision always goes in favour of divorce. There is not a single matter which remains indisposed. All matters are disposed and all are divorced. This is the bitter truth of the world.
AMOL:	It means now you are agreed that all are the same?
TARA:	Of course. All are same.
AMOL:	My dad also says the same.
TARA:	He says that nothing is new in this regard. All is said and old. All know it. All embrace it happily or unhappily. No one can get out of its clutch – the eternal clutch of 'zero into four'.
AMOL:	[Weeps] But I want to see my mother. I really want to meet my mother.
TARA:	All meet their mother. Let the time come. Definitely, all meet. All are welcome. The eternal mother never forgets anyone. She is always ready to welcome anyone according to time, place and action.
JAMES:	I meet my mother daily.
TARA:	Right you are. Let the time come, all meet her. She is one hundred per cent impartial. She is very honest and sincere.
JAMES:	She gives me toffees and biscuits – she gives me food and garments. This garment has been bought for me by her. [shows garments]

TARA:	She gives us everything.
AMOL:	I know that mother is a lie who sinks very easily like the sun in the evening. No one should expect anything from her. Everything is time-bound.
JAMES:	But my mother is the heaven of heavens, full of love and mercy for me. All mothers in my village are the same. All believe the same. We all regard them well. There is a very familiar song in my village which is sung by villagers and which is very common. We use to sing it very happily.
AMOL:	Which song?
JAMES:	'Mother is full of love ...'
AMOL:	Can you sing it?
JAMES:	Yes.
AMOL:	Please sing it.
JAMES:	Okay. Listen.

[sings] Mother is full of love –
Compassions in her grove.
Her lap is far greater
Than the heaven's shelter –
Equal to a million nurses
With all heavenly verses.

Mother is replaced by none,
Full of values and virtues.
All may become an enemy
The mother gives us honey.
In life others may hate
But she wants to see us great.

AMOL:	[laughingly] All sing. All become its victims.
JAMES:	You are prejudiced. You are a mother-hater because you have been divorced by your mother.
AMOL:	No, that is not the matter.
JAMES:	It is the fact you should realise.

AMOL: No. I am not a mother-hater. I have a sense of true respect and love for her.

JAMES: You are now unjust.

AMOL: Believe me. I am always just. I say what I see. I can show you many things in proof, if you come to my home tomorrow or you call me to your home.

JAMES: Okay. I invite you to come to my home tomorrow.

AMOL: Okay.

JAMES: You will be flooded with motherly love in my home. I will tell my mother to adopt you as a son, and you will forget your woes and sorrows.

AMOL: Thanks a lot, my friend. Thanks a lot my brother. I will come to your home tomorrow.

JAMES: My pleasure.

Lights down.

Act 3

Lights up.

AMOL arrives at JAMES' home. He sits on a chair discussing the topic of mother.

JAMES: Most welcome!

AMOL: Thanks a lot, my friend.

JAMES: How are you, friend?

AMOL: Anyway ... fine.

JAMES: Anything new?

AMOL: No.

JAMES: I am happy seeing you in my home.

AMOL: My pleasure. Where is your mother?

JAMES: My mother has gone to city.

AMOL: Why?

JAMES: Shopping ... for official works. She doesn't tell me exactly.

AMOL: Why?

JAMES: She frequently goes when I am at school and when my dad is in the office. Sometimes, my dad goes with her.

AMOL: [*Long pause*] Why?

JAMES: I don't know.

AMOL: You must know.

JAMES: I ask them but they say I am a child and I needn't know.

AMOL: [*very sad*] Oh! Oh! Very tragic! The same was said to me by my dad and mother and once she divorced me – she divorced my dad. We are now alone. The same tragedy will occur to you. I am sure.

~ 34~

JAMES:	Have you gone mad?
AMOL:	Are you not able to accept the bitter truth of life?
JAMES:	What do you say now? Have you gone mad?
AMOL:	Wait for some time.
JAMES:	What do you like to say?
AMOL:	Your condition is the same as mine. This is the process of divorce. All pass in the same way. This is the way adopted by all.
JAMES:	My friend, my situation is different. We all are happy. We all live together and enjoy our life happily. It seems we are in the heaven of heavens – equal to ten thousand heavens.
AMOL:	You are entirely in a state of illusion. I can say nothing to you. You have to understand yourself. [begins to weep.]
JAMES:	Why are you weeping, my brother?
AMOL:	[Weeping] Once, you will be also divorced. I expect it soon.
JAMES:	How?
AMOL:	[Weeping] In the same way, my brother.
JAMES:	God will not let it happen. Keep silent. I will help you. My mother will love you. My mother will adopt you too.
AMOL:	Thanks, my friend. But ...
JAMES:	What?
AMOL:	Only the earth mother adopts us. All divorce. [weeps. Tears in eyes.]
JAMES:	Keep silent, my brother. I will keep you with me. Let my mother come from her outing. She will adopt you.
AMOL:	[Weeps]
JAMES:	Please ... my brother ... keep patience.

AMOL: [*Weeping*] All keep patience as they have no option except this.

JAMES: Keep silent.

AMOL: [*Silent, sad*]

JAMES: [*Long pause*] Have you brought the proof here?

AMOL: Yes.

JAMES: Please show me the proof which you told me about yesterday.

AMOL: Okay.

JAMES: Come on, hurry up.

AMOL: See all this. The wallet is full of such documents.

JAMES: Very good. Show me one by one.

AMOL: See.

JAMES: A number of documents.

AMOL: Yes.

JAMES: It will take time.

AMOL: Yes.

JAMES: Are these of your dad?

AMOL: Yes. He has deeply studied the cases of divorce. He is an expert. He has collected several records. His diary is also full. He says that no one can change his findings because his ideas are based on several research papers.

JAMES: But my dad doesn't keep such thing. He tells my mother to keep the house clean and maintain its holiness and affinity. My mother happily does so. She is very happy doing so.

AMOL: I can show you several research works in where it has been mentioned that there are one hundred per cent divorcees in the world. The family is destroyed badly. There is control by none over anyone. All fail to control such happenings.

JAMES: But I do not agree with this point that all mothers are the same and they have no love.

AMOL: I am right because my findings are based on research. Believe.

JAMES: Believe me!

AMOL: I know all this well.

JAMES: All mothers are not the same. My mother is full of love and mercy for me and for my brothers and sisters too. She remains hungry when we fall ill. She doesn't eat when she will not see us. She waits for us till we return home from school.

AMOL: Believe me, all are the same. See the data published in the magazines. Sixty per cent of children are mother-less. Thirty of twenty per cent of children are father-less. Ten per cent of children are parentless. All are one hundred per cent in the same condition.

JAMES: [silent]

AMOL: You can imagine the world and its situation. My dad is a specialist. All articles have been collected and kept safe. He says that all are the same and this is not a matter of shame or suffering.

JAMES: How?

AMOL: [show] See and understand. See this data published in magazines in which all this is obviously mentioned. It is based on a survey by the supreme organization of the world. All are unhappy.

JAMES: [silent]

AMOL: All weep. All suffer. All are dry. No mercy to them – no love to them – no compassion to them for their children. All follow 'zero into four'.

JAMES: But know. My mother is quite different.

AMOL: There are thousands of research papers which are full of such news and research which reveals that there is no love by any mother and they divorce not only their husbands but also their children. They say they are virgin. They are unmarried. It means to say they feel their children are burdens on their heads. So, they don't like to be recognised by their children.

JAMES: No ... no.

AMOL: What?

JAMES: You are abandoned from motherly love, so you have lost faith in your mother.

AMOL: No ... no.

JAMES: Listen to me.

AMOL: Say.

JAMES: [show] There are dozens of clothes which have been bought by her for me. It shows her love for me. Think about my mother.

AMOL: It is quite false. Let the time come. Soon, everything will be gone.

JAMES: My mother too?

AMOL: Yes ... yes.

JAMES: Impossible.

AMOL: Easily possible. All do. She will do the same. New babies will replace you. New uncles will replace your dad.

JAMES: Stupid ideas.

AMOL: It is too bitter, but the eternal truth. No one wants to listen to this fact.

JAMES: Quite stupid.

AMOL: Read such news articles. Their children also said and believed that their mothers loved them but they were divorced and now they are motherless. Mothers are always the cause of change and upheaval.

JAMES: No.

AMOL: Believe it. Her shape changes like the earth mother. The earth mother is their look.

JAMES: Stupid ideas.

AMOL: All live in a state of confusion and illusion, and soon everything gets out of hand. You must admit that which is natural – which is an eternal fact.

JAMES: I can never accept that which is meaningless.

AMOL: Believe, my friend. The concept of mother and motherhood is quite meaningless. There is nothing in its name. It is a false concept. All are commanded by the formula of 'zero into four'.

JAMES: Stupidity in all research papers. Throw them away and learn to respect and love mother.

AMOL: Believe it! Believe me! All this is based on the research of scholars. Some people say mothers are godesses.

JAMES: Do you say?

AMOL: All say.

JAMES: I believe that mother is the only truth and all others are false. All are illusions.

AMOL: I know well its reality.

JAMES: No one knows the values of mother.

[JAMES' mother, ZARA returns from an outing. JAMES and AMOL greet her. She blesses them and sits on a chair. JAMES is happy seeing her. AMOL is also happy. She gives them toffees. They eat and thank her.]

ZARA: Take toffees and biscuits, my dear sons.

JAMES: Thanks mama!

AMOL: Thanks mama!

ZARA: How are you, my sons?

JAMES: Very good!

AMOL: Nice!

ZARA: Eat toffees and biscuits. [She goes to the inner part of her house for a bit. Comes back with a briefcase full of garments and some other materials. She sits in a serious mood.]

JAMES:	Why have you brought a briefcase, mama?
ZARA:	[*silent*]
JAMES:	Why? Mama … mama.
ZARA:	[*silent*]
AMOL:	My aunt, tell him.
JAMES:	Tell me, mama.
ZARA:	[*Goes to* JAMES *and kisses him.*] I love you, my heart-beat – I love you my blood-bit. When the time comes, I will welcome you. Care for yourself. Your father will guide you. Your father will look after you.
JAMES:	[*restlessly*] What? What? What … mama?
AMOL:	[*astonishingly*] Annihilation … annihilation!
JAMES:	[*restlessly*] What? Tell me, mama.
ZARA:	I am going.
JAMES:	[*restlessly*] Where?
ZARA:	The uncle is waiting for me outside our home.
JAMES:	[*restlessly*] Who?
ZARA:	A new uncle. The pet dog will also go with me.
JAMES:	[*restlessly*] Will you go with him?
ZARA:	Yes.
JAMES:	[*restlessly*] When will you come back?
ZARA:	I will welcome you.
JAMES:	[*restlessly*] It means I will come to you?
ZARA:	Yes.
JAMES:	You will not come to me?
ZARA:	No. This is the universal truth. So, you will have to follow it.
JAMES:	[*restlessly*] It means you are leaving me – you are divorcing me and my dad?
ZARA:	[*Kissing. Speaks slowly. Starts to leave.*] Yes.

JAMES: [*Begins to weep bitterly. Clasps her feet.*] I will die. My dad will die. How will I live? How will we live? My mother ... don't divorce me ... don't leave me ... don't leave us ... mama ... mama.

AMOL: [*Restlessly. Begins to weep bitterly. Clasps her feet.*] Aunt ... aunt ... don't leave us ... don't divorce us ... you are our mother ... you are full of love and mercy ... don't go ... aunt ... aunt ... we will die.

ZARA: [*Tries to be free from their clutches.*] Leave my feet. Let me go. The uncle is waiting outside. Your father will care for you.

AMOL: [*Weeps bitterly. Clasps her feet.*] Don't leave us ... don't divorce us.

JAMES: [*Weeps bitterly. Clasps her feet.*] Don't leave us ... don't divorce us.

ZARA: [*Tries to be free from their clutches. Forcibly.*] I can't stay. This is the order of the supreme agency. None can cancel this order. I am unable to disregard this order. None can disregard the system of 'zero into four'.

ZARA breaks free and leaves them weeping and rolling on the floor. She calls her pet dog but it turns its face and doesn't go.

The song 'Life is zero into four ...' is heard from an unknown direction.

Life is zero into four,
For gaining all woes here,
Moving on thorns' to boo,
Beaten by flowers too.

Life is zero into four,
For the world as all are
All use to sing the same,
Feeling that it is fame.

Life is zero into four,
The world abuses ever.
All blast this short fuse –
Showing a short amuse.

Lights down.